EUPHONY

EUPHONY

✦

Bo Crowder

OFFA'S PRESS
2016

OFFA'S PRESS

First published in 2016 by Offa's Press,
Ferndale, Pant, Oswestry, Shropshire, SY10 9QD.

ISBN: 978-0-9955225-2-7

Typeset in Baskerville Old Face
Designed by Marie Jones, printed and bound by Lion FPG Limited,
Oldbury Road, West Bromwich, B70 9DQ.

Contents

Apedale	7
Contagious Magic	8
Euphony	9
Fly Fishing in Dovedale	10
Grand	11
Hand Made	12
Happiness	13
House Clearance	14
Keggy Hand	15
MinE	16
Mother's day	17
Museum Hare	18
Pa55w0rd	19
Palimpsest	21
Pension Day	22
Power Take Off	24
Serious Play/ Silverfish	26
Stonewall	27
Swimmer	28
The Caterpillar Club	29
The Last Pass of the 'Coronation Scot'	30
The Myth of Sisyphus	31
The Saggar Maker's Bottom Knocker (A Salutation)	32
Ubbe Iwerk's Revenge	33
Unfinished Business	35
Ursa Major	36

Acknowledgement

'Euphony' appeared in *The Poetry of Staffordshire*,
Offa's Press, 2015.

Dedication

For Susan
My new-found-land.

Big thanks to John McAuliffe, Vona Groarke,
Jeanette Winterson, F.J. (John) Williams, Simon Fletcher,
Stoke Stanza, After School Poets and Suex.

Apedale

We cross the field ignore the bull
up the hill by happy Hampton's farm
pass the primary school
shut since Podmore set the fire

through the wire over the top
we enter cold metalic hulks
semi-somnambulant shapes
moving again in the mind

squint shout an order
bellow an echo of chaos
we hold on to breath in their bowels
rattle a can into an empty breech

sun sounds the retreat
releases dark fear
dims imagination
we edge toward reality

in the distance stands a coal black pyramid a parody of Cairo
the only clue a chimney stack and cows cudding under cool trees.

Contagious Magic

We eat Muldoon
for supper,
he ate Heaney
for lunch
who gobbled Yeats
for breakfast.
Yeats nibbled Blake and
Blake chewed on Milton,
who realised that paradise was lost
when Eve bit into the first pome.

Euphony

Five hills of home
My Rome
My funny Palatine
To which all roads,
My road at any road,
Lead me to mine
Sound of my past
My gone too fast
My kin my folk
My cake of oat
Lump in my throat
My own
My Stoke

Arnold Bennett (1867-1931), Stoke author of Anna of the Five Towns among other 'local' novels, believed 'Five Towns' to be more euphonic than 'Six'.

Fly Fishing in Dovedale

There's no mutter or mumble here
the river keeps her secrets under rocks
whispers watch out to the trout
as we creep along the path
ov er th e st e pp ing st on es
as far as lovers leap where we slip away
under the soft surplus of a drooping elder
and duck down to the black backwashed pools.

The stream flows fast as we cast across
a genuflected drop, a blessing of ribboned curls,
we prey all day but catch only branches of birch.
Empty as our keep nets are
we keep our thoughts to ourselves
until the hours make the mood dull.

Stopped on the long slope home by a call
a dipper preaches on a rock, takes our confession
then bobs a bow and dives, shows how it's done.
His white bib flashes in the last peep
of the sun dropping over Thorpe Cloud
blinding us with his trick in the water.

Blinking in a nave between the hills
we feel like men of fish, angled by angels.

Grand

The empty house waits
wanting the return of the flat capped hero
whose mask never slips
and his side kick Tonto,
you hobnail down the entry
and I skip to the door.

With chairs drawn up
chapped knees cry out
seams hiss steam
and black sweet tea,
saucers past parched lips,
loosens your tongue,
whets my appetite.

Then grand words
fall, like the pennies
from your pockets
when you walked on hands
down the yard,
and I can keep
all I catch.

Hand Made

We renovate this old barn
with our own hands, scutching off
strapping and mixing the lime
mortar to make black flecks shine,
like dark stars in milky lines,
between rough gritstone quoins.

We dig out the floor and drop
the level, more than a foot,
stripped to shorts and boots, bare backed,
sweating through the summer, mark
our dusty calloused palms, see
the pile of tea bag slops.

Last we lift the tiles, burnt orange
terracotta, and place them
to lean safe against a wall,
check the purlins, rafters, joists
and put the tiles back one by
one, scrap the chipped and cracked.

Sorting the duds, *my job*, on
the obverse of one I find
an imprint, hard to see except
by slanted light. Look! A child's
hand impressed in clay, I keep
this tile and throw the rest away.

Happiness

Rosebud,
good News at Ten, a half volley,
autumn rust, a nutmeg, swallows on a chat line,
cudding cows, an underdraft, a pile-ironed,
a glass half full, a tree too fat to hug,
silent shop assistants, dumb barbers, sleeping children,
a tamed tongue twister, clear roads,
a lie in on a weekday, tracks in a snowfield-yours,
a white spot on a white wall, a Tequila sunset,
a walking dog, total silence, a day at the hoe face,
popcorn in the dark, a horse galloping in the opposite direction,
an empty beach, Jameson's meets Montecristo.

House Clearance

The *tranclements* clutter
the kitchen, a brass ashtray
with the final fag, false teeth
for the Queen's speech, the toasting fork
crusted with crumbs, shellac 78's
all shook up in a box,
six pairs of spectacles
each one focussed on an age.
The *back kitchen,* only she
still has one, now it is cold
cleared of all but the cooker…
rings of rust top it, she was
immoveable too. Besides,
most of what was
precious she gave away,
pig headedness is
in the will and I'll be sure
to inherit that.

Keggy Hand

I'm trying to keep the lines straight, I do my very best.
A lawn's a curse or a blessing, depending on your point of view
and when the sun is setting and there's trouble with the kids-
they've been promised a game - better be the keeper
of that promise. Hurry if they catch you out even once,
for sure they have long memories is all I'm saying.
I take the clippings up to the compost and bury
my head in the bucket and dig out all that mulchy
green, summer absinthe, and I know buried in there
somewhere is another kid nagging for a game.

'Lord Ted does it this way,' you say and I'm watching
and trying and you say 'those born to play are
dextrous.' Awkward, keggy handed, I stick it out.
Mirrored as I am I observe the grip, the stance, the stroke
and do my very best. I stand at the crease, a cracked slab,
you bowl slow balls at first, and gradually I get it,
a sweep to the covers, the drainpipe,
a glance to the slips, the kitchen window, or
a drive through your legs for four, the yard gate.
These boundaries, it's fun to slam the ball
at them, they're all made up for me you say, I think I see
the real pitch and me at the middle of a great green oval,
you've been there. Sometimes I miss the swing completely,
but sometimes I smack one in the centre and there's a sweet
sound and that feeling of connection. Gradually I get it.
It's six and out, you say and don't forget it.

The lawn is smooth; the lines are straight, well straight enough.
The buzz of the mower has become a busy whine
- the kids, I've promised them a game.
I get the bat and ball and show them the right way
to knock the stumps in, with the handle, but it's awkward
so I let them find their own way and sod Lord Ted –

they use the face, leave dents in it, add some to mine.
We spend a long time deciding what the rules are
and the game itself seems to be over before it's begun.
Just enough time to wash our hands before tea.

MinE

My art is a bed, made of unbroken thought,
my heart is a bed of broken promises,
your thoughts are made to lie in bed with you.
Promise you'll lie beside me in your bed,
as I lie about you when I am in my bed.
Besides my bed is made and, when I lie in it,
I think of an unmade bed and of my art.

Mother's Day

They sit and knit a memory
she lifts a cigarette, he lights,
inhale, a glowing tip, exhale,
that's how contractions are controlled.

He smiles, her laugh accelerates
she finishes his sentences
inside each fold of skin she holds
a year for each of hers and his.

The cigarette has burned down to a nub,
the fading light signals the time to go,
he stands shrugs on his coat and hesitates,
Do come again, she says in the 'Queen's Own'.

He gives her crumpled shell a quick embrace,
she blows a kiss, an O into the air,
            and grinds the butt; for ash is all there is.

Museum Hare

I know you sprinter renewable
Spirit of spring nip in the bud

Once you ran as ziggger- zagger
Unwatchable uncatchable

Give us a lovesick kiss for summer
Before the heat encloses the hum

Hover over every lover
Shadow us in your moonlight night

Between soil and sky we shiver
Waiting for you to dance anew

Brown on the down earth echo
Boxer doe or lucky buck

Totem brother oestrus form
Race again and start the stars

Still time in us to see your speed
Deep within you live you live

Locked alone you cannot answer
Sad dash spirit wreck of the road

Dead entertainer dead educator
Door-nail dead you lay you lie.

Pa55w0rd

Don't panic
No that's not it
Only an open mind
Can close in on the answer
#? That's a joke
I gave them up years ago
Mmm …Must have at least eight parts
The secret is to avoid
Getting hacked off
Try closing the eyes
Is it a pet?
Never had any
A place I am drawn to?
Page 404 error not found
My first school?
I'd rather not go there
It's a memory act
A virtual post it note
Three wishes
Equal to…success

I'm so happy that you're made up
You're simple and yet
Complex at the same time
Don't look so smug you can always be replaced
Does that make you insecure?
In any case I'm not faithful to you
I suppose you feel used
Because it's true I have known
Others and see many of them everyday
Are you alarmed by that?
Of course you're precious but
And here's a thinly disguised hint
Not the thing I'm most likely to grab

When running from a burning building
But you are a notable date
I love you/ hate you/ can't get you
Out of my head
You protect my crown jewels
So all's well under the sun
Forgettable that's what you are

Palimpsest

Broken in on a gravestone
by a beery breathed rough hewer of coal
grinding her into a white dust
like the clay that settled on her face
from the pots she carried to the kiln.

Black and white they were
squares on a chess board
touching yet opposed
in the beginning
equal in area.

But black ink scribbles on white paper
black hands stain white sheets
black boots stamp on white feet
so she washed the feet
shredded the sheets for rags
and screwed the paper up for kindling.

She learned to creep snore silently
lie impassive without a whimper
count the money in the wallet while he slept
the only thing they did together
was grow old.

Finally the day he heaved his last
with a wheeze the shafts collapsed
and she bent to listen as
words whispered from his lips.

They blew on the breeze
and flew through the window
she traced them with a finger
over his dead form.

Pension Day

The sky is cast, a grey metallic mass
over the pithead folding around
the hum from the winches, two
circles spinning in opposite directions.

I follow their flickering, like wagon wheels
caught back travelling in a western.

The old man's hand bent leather glove
contoured, mapped made for mine, slips
from my grasp as he stops to lean against the gate.

His lips pucker and gasp
in the close air and he plucks
a handkerchief from his hip
and coughs a scarlet apology.

When his breathing steadies we move
on up the hill, in the stillness
barely a breeze breaks
the monotony of the weekly walk.

At the boiler room we rest
to listen to the clatter of the stokers
loading coke into the fire.

The old man strokes a shovel,
like an old friend, layed up in a corner,
his movements draw smiles from the men
as they pause to nod in our direction
before turning their grunting backs.

A tap on the office window brings
the brown envelope which he signs for
with the pen layed out for the job,
tied with a string to the counter top,
it will never escape to complete a
crossword or a shopping list.

The long slow walk back down
the hill is an easier stride
to the blue tiled terraced house
held fast by neighbours back to back.

Power Take Off

He swept the old grey tractor
of cobwebs,
'my girl you should get out more'
he muttered, and pressed the starter.
As the engine stuttered
the rusty exhaust coughed
a smoky breath of black
into the air. He backed
towards the mower and
hitched her up,
he slipped the gear
P...T...O...
it moaned. Down he got
bent near its groan, still closer
just to be assured.
That rusty tractor giving you some stick?
A bright and breezy wife
has much to hide. He didn't turn,
but hairs stood on his neck,
'I don't need your help…
go inside.'
Are you still mad at me my love, my dear?
He heard the words,
inside he felt a fear that the work:
the woman: sapped
his strength, worn out,
wilted with the effort,
understanding, land is hard,
but wives are more demanding.
A farm falls to the first born
but he fell first for the farm,
full in his flesh, his bones
absorbed.

He thought it best he should not doubt
the calls, the absences,
the late nights out. She crept home
like a thistle throwing rhizomes.
Pushed to the headland
of his mind she had grown
wild, nettled, as untopped fields
are prone to do and she,
like wicked words, was not alone
for long, finding truth in lies, good in bad.
The sun had shone
for three days on the trot,
he had to cut the hay
before it shot.
He pulled the cover back
and oiled the shaft,
had her denial set his mind at rest?
A gift a trusting smile, and yet
the best of actors show or tell.
By now, her craft he recognised
as rot, a spoiled sack. Her words-
No I never,
- echoed hollow. Truth
from lips so quick to melt,
slow to crack, was like a running hare,
too hard to follow. Just then she kissed him
and in his ear let slip,
Your overalls are worn, I'll stitch you up
And carefully she tore
a hefty rip, to dangle down,
He never saw it drop, as he leaned
by that spinning shaft,
she reckoned,
Six feet of farmer, wrapped up in a second.

Serious Play

…obsesses me from blink awake to last lids.
Left alone it hums, it squeaks,
it sparks, it grates, it shouts,
it speaks, it sings, it whispers and it nags,
trembles down the arm into the hand, finding
a space outside one universe, inside another.

The American poet Robert Frost, (1874-1963),
considered poetry 'serious play'.

Silverfish

Bunk bed, pillow fight, Beano and Dandy swap,
fried bread, football, sweat, dog shit, gravel rash,
dare, truth, kiss, command or promise, bobby's hat,
grass stains, Park Drive, shut shops, cabbage water,
thumb twiddle, Family Favourites, roast potatoes, mash,
pub, bar, beer, piss, pop, shoulder, home,
Yorkshire Pudding, beef, shandy, belly ache, boredom,
back lane, entry, echo, latch, carbolic soap,
card games, Songs of Praise, chenille tablecloth,
tinned salmon, tinned pears, brown bread and butter,
Tizer, Guinness, froth, Old Twist, clothes horse,
rag-rug, silverfish, toasted currant bun,
coal, fire, spit, smoke, cough, Zed Bed,
pearls, Eau de Cologne, medicine, walking stick,
Bible, bath, bed, flashing blue light, knock.

Stonewall

I am millstone-grit
piled in a stack
nodding in the wind,
rain rasped, stood
for a hundred years
rocked by moles and the
blast from the quarry down the road.

Leaning on mildewed gateposts
propped up by strainers
in the corner,
nothing moves me like
the tear of a tongue on the swarth
or a sweet arsed pony
rubbing me up the wrong way.

If I fail, unable to cope,
put me back in the right place.

Swimmer

We are not enemies
although she seduced him

hold no grudge against me

see him dip in and out
of her flush her through
his fingers
young gangling

I worship his feet
fill his nostrils with sweet
sun dried scent
suck at him
clammy slap
fold around him,
caress and clutch

see her mock
his unfamiliar movements

conscious unconscious

he feels the warm touch
of a friendly face

buoyed boy

but she is cool
and cold down below

I tug at his hips

shrug her off
push her away

when he sleeps
he dreams of her
tomorrow
he will go back to her.

The Caterpillar Club

'life depends on a silken thread.'

90 years old and he's forgotten what he said only moments ago.
Was he sitting in the tail flying backwards?
He remembers the training, take-off and landing, gun practice,
recalls the presence of the land lit only
by the dull red glow of incendiaries.
He hears the banter of the crew as they corkscrew to canon fire,
sees the length of flame from the port engine,
feels the slipstream, the floating, the fall,
smells the field of corn, lies in the silence of the earth.
He can nag for bread in four languages,
brot bitte, khleb pozhaluysta, du pain, toast.
He says it again,
I wish I could bail out.

The Last Pass of the 'Coronation Scot'

Let's go for a walk, she says holding out
her hand. I take it and stand, my legs

are weak, my mouth is dry, the still air closing
in on us as we pass under trees

and move together deeper into the wild wood.
Dappled shadows, light playing on the trickling

stream, the fetid smell of leaf mould and
fungus, green moss covered fallen branches

cracking, grassy slopes sliding under foot,
sticky hands clamped together, silk shoulders

slipping under fingers, inhale, fragrance, muted leaves
rustling around the ground, crumpled, a taste on the tip

of the tongue, hesitant echoes drifting
through the air, a cry, a sigh, exhale, still,

two hearts beating in time to the swinging
bluebell blanket floor, she whispers, *listen… a whistle.*

The Myth of Sisyphus

'one must imagine (him) happy' Albert Camus

I met Sisyphus propping up the bar
after a long day's shove and he said,

Look at my busted hands.

Don't they let you wear gloves?

Not only do they not issue protective hand wear,
They didn't carry out a risk assessment either.

He sank a Bourbon, blinked at the barmaid
and made a pass at the bartender

Why don't you complain?

It's a Zeus-hours contract, I might lose my position.

Are you happy pushing that rock up a hill every day?

He paused to light a cigarette and looked so self-possessed
I could have sworn a Greek god had descended from Olympus.

It's not the pushing of the rock up the hill that's important,
It's the long walk down the other side to fetch it again…
it gives me time to think.
I mean…what if it's the wrong rock?

The Saggar Maker's Bottom Knocker
(A Salutation)

Dusty lad 'prentice to a 'prentice
in whose hand the mawl falls flat and even,
cocked cap hero who makes piecework
at odds with clock and clay
watchful of breaks in the saggar's base
up before the crack of dawn,
snacks on cold snappin' and a cool pint
to slake away cough and kiln.

How should we salute you?

Cold shadow, cast across five towns
you jiggered us to what we are, your ware
filled the world's tables, fed our mouths,
your slip made us aspire to be the best, you
branded us as a place to come from,
though you became a what's my line?
A silly name to shout, lungs out of breath,
'China made in England.'

Ubbe Iwerk's Revenge

Last night I slept with Minnie Mouse.
As mice go I wouldn't say she was
unattractive.
I fell for her eyes, black pools with
long slender lashes set off by
a carefully applied pale blue eye shadow.
There were the big ears and the buck teeth to contend
with
but who worries about these things
in the heat of passion?

Everything seemed quite natural.
The wall to wall mouse droppings on the floor of her
apartment:
the bed,
a small nest of straw scraped into one corner of the room
and, when she removed her gloves,
the missing fingers.

Her tail she used as a prehensile sex aid;
it was really very stimulating.
As were those mousy little squeaks that she made,
her downy body moving underneath me with,
I have to admit,
a pleasurable reciprocity of emotion.
I do remember her breath smelt a little cheesy.

Only afterwards did I notice
all around the bed, the giant mousetraps,
haphazardly arranged,
an obstruction to the inevitable visit to the bathroom.
Putting this off,
I leaned back against the headboard,
lit a cigarette and looked at her.

On reflection,
It wasn't
casual sex with a rodent that most disturbed me.

It wasn't
the way I savoured my cigarette
in what was, frankly,
an impossibly cinematic way.
It was
when I asked, in Walt's distinctive falsetto,

'How was it for you baby?'

Ubbe Iwerks was an animator and special-effects man who, together with his more famous partner Walt Disney, created the cartoon character Mickey Mouse.

Unfinished Business

They have come away on holiday, bringing the box they were unable to unpack.
Oh to escape the sink hole of the suburbs for one weekend.

At the entrance to the boathouse an oversized key half hides behind a pottery pig,
a yellow rose bush fringes the threshold.

The fresh paint stings their nostrils as they enter the hall, it lies over the fetid
corners and inside the dank gable closets.

They dump the bags on the bed, ignore the complaining floor and cross through
the double doors: out and onto the balcony.

The river slides slowly past, a floating mass carrying the jetsam of the land along,
half- submerged logs, junk, sea swallow.

He throws his thoughts as far as the furthest bank as she drops hers into the flow,
sentencing them to downstream.

He drifts into the kitchen and runs a guzzle of water into the kettle, flicks the gas
on high and scratches the base across the griddle.

She cracks the suitcase locks, tips the clothes onto the bed and stacks her own
neatly into a drawer, thunking it shut with a knee.

The kettle blows, he pours, he sweetens, he stirs, and hands her a mug. They
sip steaming tea together, eyes docked.

She unhooks her bra, shrugs her shoulders out of the straps, slides her hand up
a sleeve and produces a white flag in her fingers.

At home, the unfinished business, lurks in the dark corners of the house, hidden
in the sheets, holed up in the bottom of the laundry basket.

Ursa Major

That looks nothing like a bear, you say
as we lie in the open staring at stars
trying out our Greek eyes with this
blackety black point to point puzzle.

The truckle beds are uncomfortable,
we are not in a double, you want me
like a spoon, there's an itch to know other,
what's that crawling up my leg?

We eat almonds slowly, bursting
soft green shells with a thumbnail,
the fire spits red dwarfs,
glowing flotsam in the air.

I explain what a light year is
six million million miles of
speed bumps and give way signs,
I'm not counting.

Warm beer, cool air, we bounce
ideas off satellites
as they join the dots for us,
I need to touch you.

From separate beds we reach out,
as our fingertips meet a static spark,
a free of charge that we unearthed,
makes a moment into a universe.

In answer a meteorite flashes
in the corner of my eye, synapses
snap their fingers at each other,
looks more like a saucepan to me.

A thought we cook a little
and then stare some more,
inside our heads a black hole
sucks at everything.